KU-610-712

CONTENTS

What is a Flea? 4

A Flea Up Close 6

Hairy Homes 8

Blood Sucking 10

Passing It On 12

Waiting for a New Home 14

Biggest Jumper 16

Scattered Eggs 18

Detecting a Host 20

Fleas & Humans 22

Bloodsucking Relatives 24

More Bloodsuckers 26

Life Cycle and Fabulous Facts 28

Glossary 30

Index 32

What is a Flea?

Fleas are small, wingless insects. They are so small they are hard to see. Fleas can jump amazing distances… and they bite!

Bats can have lots of fleas, as the fleas can spread easily when the bats are roosting.

How do they live?

Fleas feed on blood, but they are not predators. Predators kill their prey before feeding, but fleas take their blood from living victims. Creatures like the flea, which feed off the living bodies of other creatures, are known as parasites.

4

minibeasts

Flea's new home

Clint Twist

Copyright © ticktock Entertainment Ltd 2006

First published in Great Britain in 2006 by ticktock Media Ltd.,

Unit 2, Orchard Business Centre, North Farm Road, Tunbridge Wells, Kent, TN2 3XF

ISBN 1 86007 841 9 PB Printed in China

A CIP catalogue record for this book is available from the British Library.

Picture Credits

Alamy: 1, 8 (Papilio), 6, 9, 21t (PHOTOTAKE Inc), 6-7 (M I (Spike) Walker), 8-9 (Juniors Bildarchiv), 15t (imagestopshop), 23 (Jack Sullivan). Ardea: 21 side panel (Steve Hopkin). Bananastock: 16-17. Corbis: 12-13 (CDC/Phil). FLPA: 7 (Albert Mans/Foto Natura), 22b (Heidi & Hans-Juergen Koch/Minden Pictures). Getty Images: 17t (Image Makers). NHPA: 1, 14 (Stephen Dalton). OSF: 12. Science Photo Library: 9 side panel (CNRI), 10 (Volker Steger), 11t (Dr P. Marazzi), 11b, 11 side panel, 18t, 18b, 19, 20b, 20-21 (K.H. Kjeldsen), 13 side panel (Martyn F. Chillmaid), 19 side panel (Peter Chadwick), 24 (Eye of Science), 25t, 25b (David Scharf), 26 (VVG).

Every effort has been made to trace the copyright holders, and we apologise in advance for any unintentional omissions. We would be pleased to insert the appropriate acknowledgements in any subsequent edition of this publication.

Dogs and cats can get fleas. These fleas are on a dog's nose.

Understanding minibeasts

Insects belong to a group of minibeasts known as arthropods. Adult arthropods have jointed legs but do not have an inner skeleton made of bones. Instead, they have a tough outer "skin" called an exoskeleton. All insects have six legs when they are adults, and most also have at least one pair of wings for flying, although some have two pairs.

Where do they live?

Fleas live on the skins of mammals and birds. Animals that have parasites living on or in their bodies are known as hosts. Fleas live wherever there are mammals or birds that can be their hosts. Bats and rodents have the most fleas, while horses are nearly flea-free.

Fleas have six legs but no wings, and they belong to the insect group.

A Flea Up Close

Fleas are about 2-7 mm long and have six legs and no wings. They have the same type of body as all other adult insects, which have three parts – head, thorax, and abdomen.

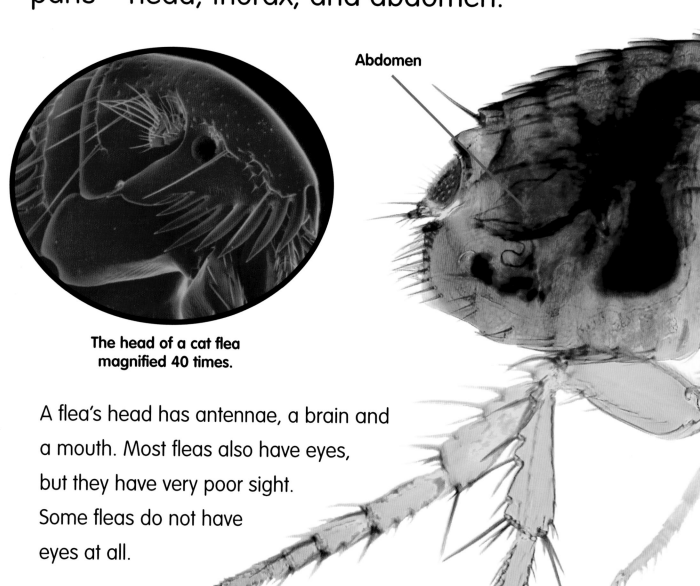

The head of a cat flea magnified 40 times.

Abdomen

A flea's head has antennae, a brain and a mouth. Most fleas also have eyes, but they have very poor sight. Some fleas do not have eyes at all.

The abdomen is largest part of the flea's body. It contains the flea's digestive system.

The thorax is the middle part of the body and the legs are attached here. The flea's back legs are longer and stronger than its front and middle legs.

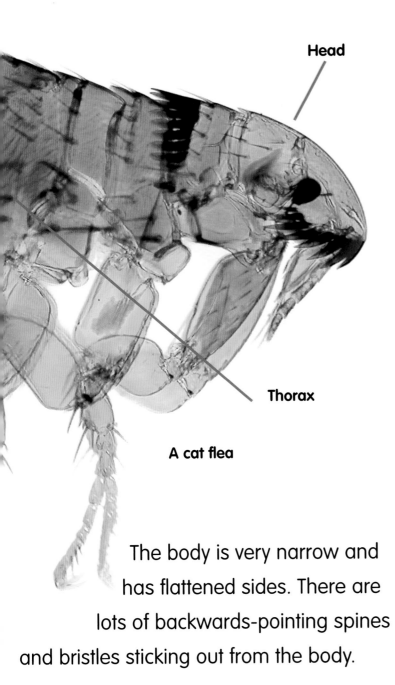

Head

Thorax

A cat flea

The body is very narrow and has flattened sides. There are lots of backwards-pointing spines and bristles sticking out from the body.

Six legs

Fleas and other insects are sometimes called hexapods because they all have six legs (hex means six in Latin). All insects are hexapods, but not all hexapods are insects. Some other minibeasts, such as springtails, have six legs but they are not true insects.

Springtails have six legs but they are not true insects. Fleas also have six legs and they are insects.

Hairy homes

A flea has tiny, sharp claws on the ends of its feet so that it can get a good grip on the soft skin of its host. A flea's narrow body makes it easy for it to move forwards between the thousands of hairs or feathers that cover the host's skin.

Mammals and birds do not like having fleas. Most mammals are constantly grooming their fur, or just scratching, to try and get rid of parasites such as fleas. Birds preen their feathers for the same reason.

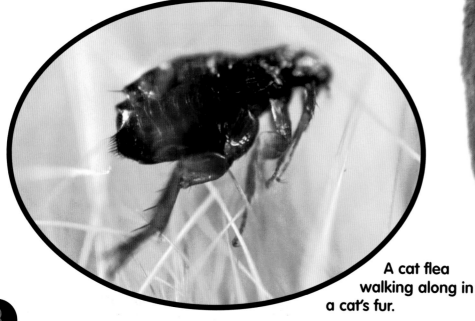

A cat flea walking along in a cat's fur.

Cat fleas have backwards pointing hairs to help them to stay on their scratching hosts.

When animals try to scratch fleas away, the bristles and spines on a flea's body become really useful. If the flea is pushed backwards, the spines and bristles catch on the host's hairs or feathers, and prevent the insect from falling off.

When a cat has fleas, it scratches and grooms itself to try and get rid of them.

On the outside

Animal parasites can be divided into two groups. Fleas, and minibeasts that live in a similar way, are known as ectoparasites because they live on the outer surface of the host. Ecto- is a scientific way of saying "external". Other minibeasts, such as tapeworms, live inside the host's body and are known as endoparasites.

Tapeworms live in fleas which are bitten off and swallowed by the host animal and settle in the digestive system.

Blood sucking

A flea's mouth is perfect for drinking blood. It has a pair of hollow, needle-like stylets that pierce the host's skin, and allow the flea to suck up warm blood.

When the flea drinks, its abdomen swells up with blood. Fleas prefer to eat once a day but, if necessary, they can go for several months without feeding.

A cat flea's head is helmet-shaped to make it easier to move through the cat's fur.

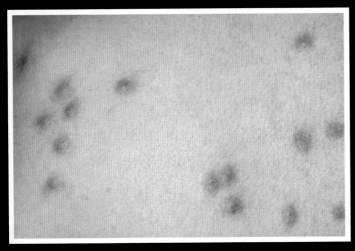

These nasty red marks are flea bites on a five-year-old child's skin.

A flea bite is almost painless, and most animals do not notice that they have been bitten at first. After a few minutes, the host's skin starts to react to substances on the flea's stylets – the bite begins to itch, and the host starts to scratch. But by this time, however, the flea has fed and moved on.

Barbed security

Flea stylets have rows of tiny, upwards-pointing barbs. If the flea is detected while it is drinking, these barbs dig into the host's flesh and make the flea very difficult to get off. Some species of fleas – the so-called "stick-tight fleas" – like to stay attached to their host's skin for days on end, holding on with these barbs.

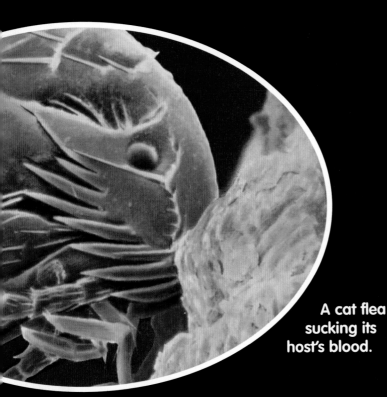

A cat flea sucking its host's blood.

The mouthparts of a cat flea. The blood-sucking stylet can be seen in the centre.

Passing it on

Unfortunately, a flea is much more than just an itchy nuisance. It can also spread deadly diseases.

Rabbit fleas, such as this one, spread the disease myxomatosis.

A single fleabite does not cause much harm by itself – the host loses a drop of blood and suffers some slight itching. The real problem is with what the flea had eaten just before.

When a flea sucks blood from a host, small traces of blood stay in its stylets. If the flea then moves to another host, those traces of blood get injected into the new host's body.

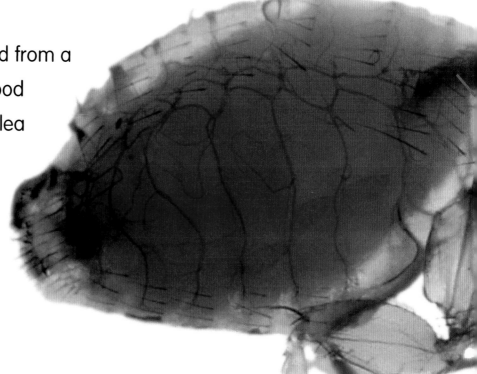

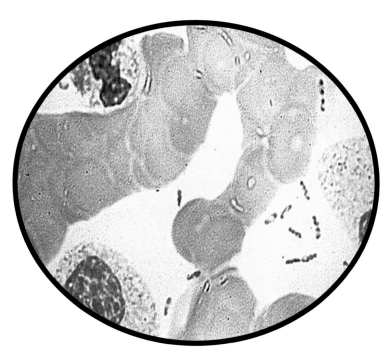

A magnified view of microbes in a drop of blood.

It is this small transfer of blood that spreads disease. If the first host has a disease, its blood will contain millions of disease-causing microbes. Even the tiny amount of blood left in a flea's stylets is enough to transfer some of these microbes into the second host. When this happens over and over again, diseases can spread very quickly.

An Oriental rat flea infected with bubonic plague, which is the dark splodge here.

Rabbit Killer

In many parts of the world rabbits are serious pests because they eat crops. In both Europe and Australia, rabbit fleas have been used to reduce the number of rabbits. A few rabbits were caught and infected with a disease called myxomatosis before being released. Rabbit fleas quickly transferred the disease from rabbit to rabbit. Within a few years, this disease killed about 95% of the rabbits.

This rabbit has red and swollen eyes which is a sign that it has myxomatosis.

Waiting for a New Home

When fleas can't find a host to live on, they can go for long periods without feeding. They can wait weeks, or even months, for the right host to come along.

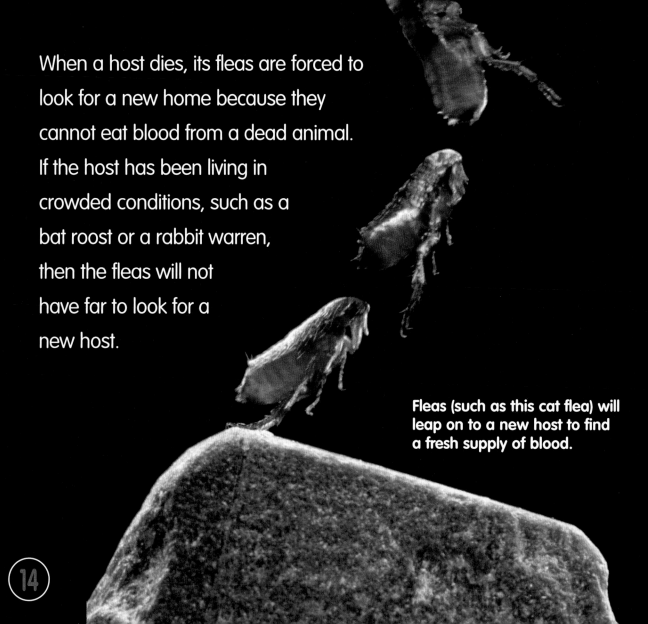

When a host dies, its fleas are forced to look for a new home because they cannot eat blood from a dead animal. If the host has been living in crowded conditions, such as a bat roost or a rabbit warren, then the fleas will not have far to look for a new host.

Fleas (such as this cat flea) will leap on to a new host to find a fresh supply of blood.

A pet cat can pass its fleas on to its owners.

f, however, the host spent a lot of its
ime on its own then the fleas may have
a long wait before a suitable host
comes close enough to jump on.

Fussy Fleas

Fleas are usually very choosy about where they live. Most flea species have a particular species of mammal or bird as their host. Rabbit fleas, for instance, will live only on rabbits, and chicken fleas will live only on chickens. Some fleas, however, are much less fussy. Cat fleas, for example, are quite happy to feed on the blood of other species, including human beings.

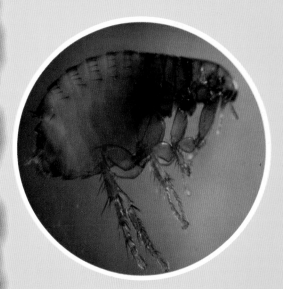

Cat fleas like this one
are not fussy and will
drink human blood.

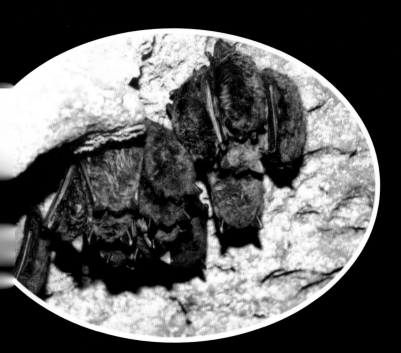

Fleas are easily passed on when
animals live close together, such
as in this bat roost.

Biggest Jumper

A flea spends most of its time either staying still, or walking slowly over the skin looking for exactly the right place to drink blood from. But when it needs to, a flea can move further and faster than any other living creature.

When escaping from its host's grooming, or just hopping aboard a new host, a flea can jump amazing distances. A flea can jump about 200 times its own body length. This is the same as a human jumping over a 40-floor skyscraper with a single leap.

When they jump, fleas accelerate more than 20 times faster than the fastest jet planes.

To jump as high as a flea, you would have to jump over a skyscraper.

Stored power

The secret of this jumping ability is in the muscles attached to the flea's long back legs. These muscles store energy in the same way that a stretched rubber band stores energy. When these muscles are triggered, they release their stored energy in one powerful burst and propel the flea high into the air.

Fleas can jump amazing distances because of the power stored in their back legs.

Scattered Eggs

Male and female fleas can only mate and reproduce if they have recently drunk fresh blood. After mating, the female flea can lay eggs as long as there is a host available with a supply of blood that she can drink every day.

Female fleas lay some of their eggs while they are feeding, and these are spread all over the host's skin.

The droppings and egg (above), and the larva (below) of a cat flea.

The eggs soon hatch into tiny larvae that are unable to drink blood like adult fleas. Instead, the larvae get their taste for blood by eating the blood-rich droppings of the adults.

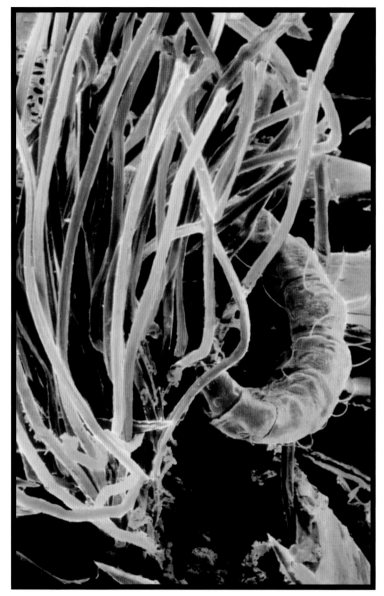

A cat flea larva in a carpet. It eats the droppings of adult fleas and will spin a cocoon. When a suitable host is nearby, it will hatch and jump on.

Insect development

Insects develop from eggs in two different ways. With many kinds of insect, including fleas, the eggs hatch into larvae that look very different from the adults. The larvae go through a stage called pupation when they change into adults. However, with many other kinds of insect, such as cockroaches and grasshoppers, the eggs hatch into nymphs that already have the adult body shape.

In less than a month, the larvae are fully grown and they pupate. Flea larvae spin themselves tiny cocoons make of a silk-like substance. Inside their cocoons, the flea pupae have to wait patiently for the right moment before emerging as adult fleas.

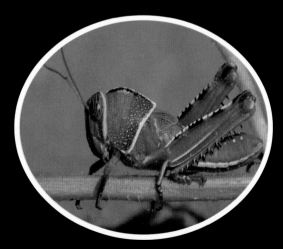

A grasshopper nymph which looks very similar to an adult grasshopper.

Detecting a Host

For fleas, pupation can take between six days to six months before the adult emerges from the cocoon. The pupa waits until a suitable host is nearby, ready for the newly emerged flea to hop aboard.

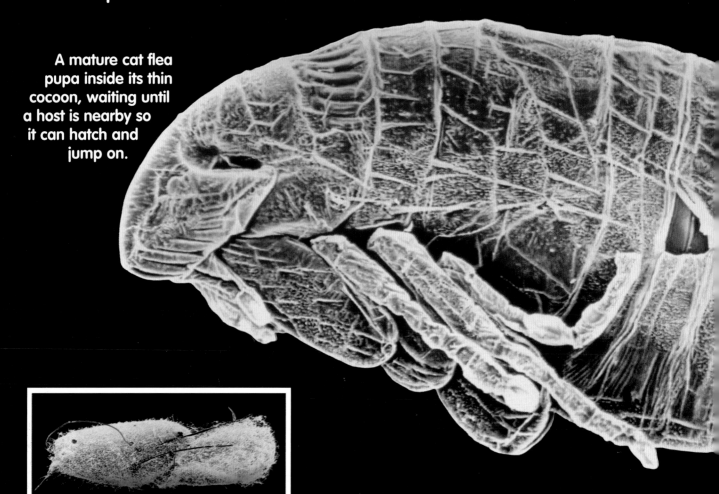

A mature cat flea pupa inside its thin cocoon, waiting until a host is nearby so it can hatch and jump on.

These are two cat flea cocoons.

When the pupa is in its cocoon, it can tell when a host is nearby but it cannot see, so it uses its other senses.

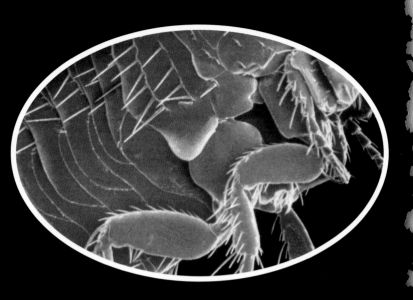

Tiny bristles on the flea's legs can sense heat and movement.

The pupa can sense its surroundings through vibration and temperature. Pupae can feel the vibrations caused by movement. They detect these vibrations through tiny bristles on their legs. Although they are tightly wrapped inside their cocoons, the vibrations caused by an animal walking nearby are enough to let the pupae know they can come out of their cocoons.

Temperature sensitive

Fleas are also very sensitive to temperature, and they can find a suitable host in complete darkness by sensing its body heat. The same is true for the pupae. When a suitable animal comes close enough that a pupa can detect its body heat, the pupation stage ends immediately. A hungry flea emerges and leaps straight at the nearest source of food, and adult life has begun.

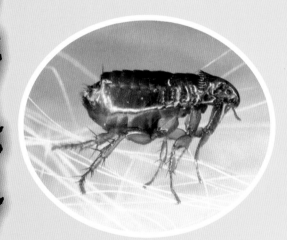

A hungry cat flea in cat fur.

Fleas & Humans

It is not surprising that human beings, who are the most widespread of all the mammals on planet Earth, should be hosts to their very own species of flea.

Human fleas are found wherever people are living in dirty and crowded conditions, especially in towns and cities. A few hundred years ago fleas were an uncomfortable part of daily life – everybody, rich or poor, had fleas.

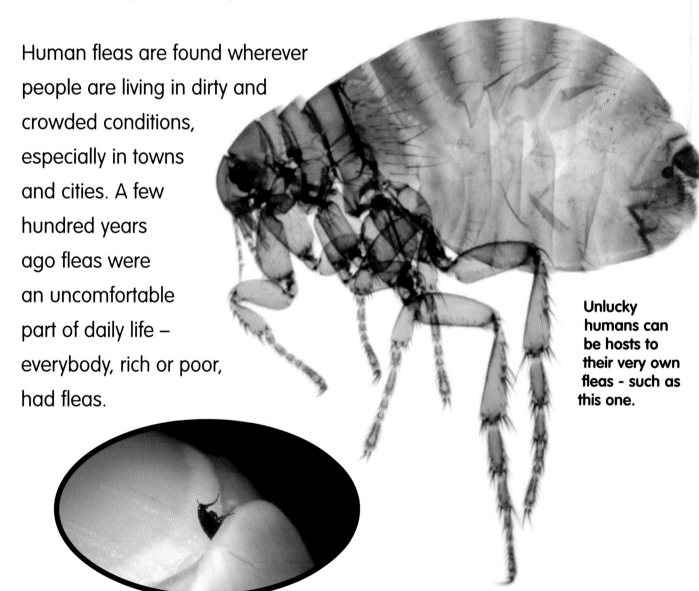

Unlucky humans can be hosts to their very own fleas - such as this one.

Fleas were once a common pest for human beings; this one is being killed between two fingernails.

Although human fleas are not as common, headlice still live on a lot of children and adults. This girl is being trated for headlice.

A fleabite swells, itches for a few days, and then disappears. The bite, in itself, does no real harm but it can result in the death of the host if the flea happens to be carrying disease-causing microbes. Fleabites can spread many dangerous human diseases, such as typhus and bubonic plague.

Black death

In the 14th Century, the Black Death (an outbreak of bubonic plague) killed one-third of Europe's population. Rat fleas carried the microbes which cause bubonic plague, and in the filthy conditions of the 14th Century, the fleas were able to spread the disease from rats to humans.

An illustration showing dead victims of the plague being collected.

Bloodsucking relatives

Fleas are a very uniform group of insects – they all look pretty much the same and behave in the same way – but there are a few confusing exceptions.

Chigoe flea

With one type of flea – the chigoe flea – the pregnant female burrows into the flesh of the host, usually in the feet. The female lives inside the flesh of the host until she is ready to lay eggs, and this causes intense itching. A chigoe flea is sometimes called a "jigger", and this is where the confusion starts.

Chigger

There is another minibeast, called a chigger, which also burrows into feet. But a chigger is not a flea, it is not even an insect. A chigger is the larva stage of certain mites that lay eggs on the ground. The eggs hatch into larvae that can bite through skin and bury themselves in the feet of animals, where they feed on their hosts' flesh. Chiggers can itch even worse than jiggers, and they both can also pass on diseases.

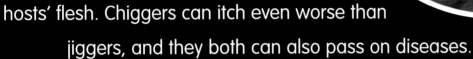

Lice

There is another group of small insects, known as lice, which also like to live on the skin of other animals. Some lice suck blood, while others do not. Bird lice, for example, usually feed on fragments of feathers. A few lice do a bird no harm, but having lots of them can cause birds to lose their feathers.

Crab louse

The crab louse is a bloodsucker that likes to live in human body hair. They have strong claws for gripping onto hairs, and females produce special glue for sticking their eggs in place. Both young and adult crab lice feed on human blood, but they are not known to carry any diseases.

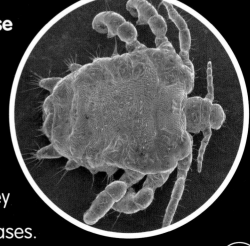

More Bloodsuckers

Many other minibeasts, as well as fleas, also live by sucking blood.

Mites

Mites are arachnids, and are related to spiders and ticks. Most mites are very small, no bigger than the thickness of a human hair. Some mites feed on plants, while others are parasites on animals of all sizes. The varroa mite, for example, is a major problem for beekeepers because the mite lays eggs inside a honeybee colony. When the young mites hatch, they feed on the honeybee larvae.

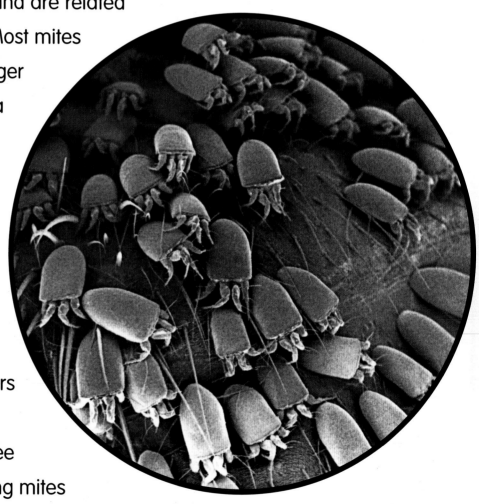

Ticks

Ticks are small arachnids, usually less than 1 cm in length, that live in much the same way as fleas. All ticks are parasites that attach themselves to a suitable host in order to suck blood. Like "stick-tight" fleas, ticks attach themselves very firmly to the host's skin. Some ticks can cause painful illnesses, such as Lyme disease.

Mosquitos

Mosquitos are small flying insects that, like fleas, have to feed on warm blood in order to breed. Mosquitoes, however, have a very different lifestyle. Their eggs are laid in still water, and the larvae hatch out as water animals – they only develop wings during pupation. Some mosquitoes carry deadly diseases such as malaria and yellow fever.

Leeches

Leeches are related to earthworms, but they live very different lives. Earthworms live in soil and eat dead plants. Leeches spend most of their time in water and feed by sucking blood from fish, amphibians, and other animals. Leeches were once widely used in medicine to remove blood from patients, and they are sometimes used today for the same purpose.

Find out More
Lifecycle

Flea eggs are white and about 0.5 mm in length. When the egg hatches (after 1-10 days) the larva emerges and feeds on adult flea droppings. After about 5-11 days, the larva will spin a cocoon and develop into the pupa. The pupa will stay in the cocoon until it senses a host nearby. When this happens, the pupa will emerge from the cocoon, leap on to the host and feast on the host's blood.

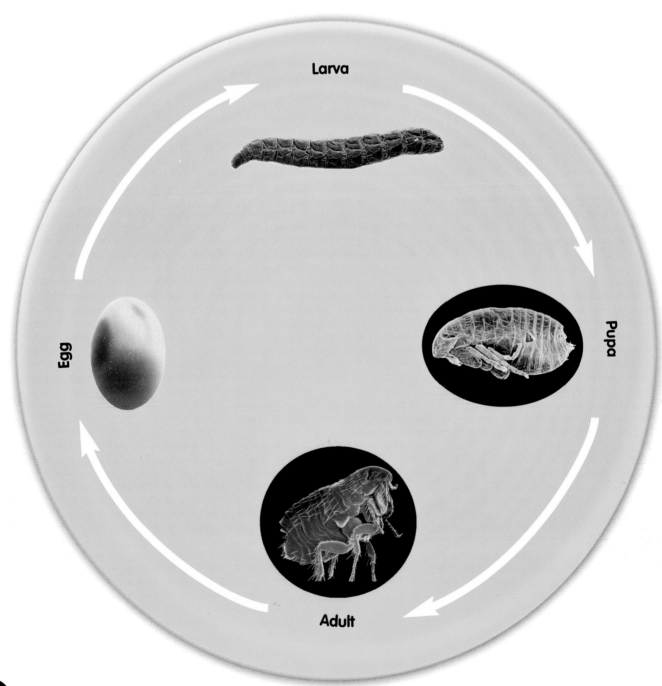

Larva

Pupa

Adult

Egg

Fabulous Facts

Fact 1: Fleas have been around for 100 million years.

Fact 2: Fleas can jump around 200 times their own length.

Fact 3: Cats and dogs can wear collars or be treated with flea-killing poison to get rid of fleas.

Fact 4: A female flea can lay about 2000 eggs in her lifetime.

Fact 5: The female flea consumes 15 times her own body weight in blood daily.

Fact 6: The flea life cycle can be completed in as little as 16 days.

Fact 7: The most common flea is the cat flea.

Fact 8: Once a pet gets fleas, its surroundings must be completely cleaned or else the pet will be re-infested.

Fact 9: A dog flea can live and breed on a dog for more than 100 days.

Fact 10: There are over 2000 species of flea.

Fact 11: Flea eggs are smooth and often fall off the host into surrounding carpets and bedding.

Fact 12: In the past, everyone had fleas but because people are cleaner now, fleas are not as common.

Fact 13: If a flea falls from its host, its tough exoskeleton will prevent it from dying on impact.

GLOSSary

Abdomen – the largest part of an insect's three-part body; the abdomen contains most of the important organs.

Acceleration – an increase in speed.

Antennae – a pair of special sense organs found at the front of the head on most insects.

Arachnid – a group of minibeasts, with four pairs of legs and a two-part body, such as spiders, mites and ticks.

Arthropod – any minibeast that has jointed legs; insects and spiders are arthropods.

Barb – a sharp point facing the opposite direction on a weapon or tool that prevents it being taken out of the victim.

Black Death – an outbreak of bubonic plague that killed about one-third of Europe's human population in the 14th Century.

Bubonic plague – a disease that normally affects wild rodents, but which can be passed onto humans by flea bites.

Cocoon – a protective covering of silk produced by some insect larvae to protect their bodies while they transform into adults.

Digestive system – the organs that are used to process food.

Ectoparasite – a parasite that lives on the outside of a host's body.

Endoparasite – a parasite that lives inside a host's body.

Exoskeleton – a hard outer covering that protects and supports the bodies of some minibeasts.

Host – an animal that can provide food and a home for parasites.

Insect – a kind of minibeast that has six legs, most insects also have wings.

Larva – a wormlike creature that is the juvenile (young) stage in the life cycle of many insects.

Lice – a group of small insect parasites often found on birds and mammals; some lice suck blood, some feed on dead skin.

Mammal – one of a group of warm-blooded animals that have an internal skeleton and which feed their young on milk.

Microbes – tiny living things, so small that they can only been seen through a powerful microscope.

Minibeast – one of a large number of small land animals that do not have a skeleton.

Myxomatosis – a disease of rabbits that is caused by microbes that can be passed on by rabbit fleas.

Nymph – the juvenile (young) stage in the life cycle of insects that do not produce larvae.

Parasite – any living thing that lives or feeds on or in the body of another living thing.

Pupa – an insect larva that is in the process of turning into an adult.

Pupation – the process by which insect larvae change their body shape to the adult form.

Rodents – a group of small mammals that includes rats and mice, but not rabbits or shrews.

Roost – a resting or sleeping place used by birds and bats.

Skeleton – an internal structure of bones that supports the bodies of large animals such as mammals, reptiles, and fish.

Springtail – a six-legged minibeast which is not an insect as it does not share the same DNA.

Stylets – the hollow, pointed parts of a flea's mouth that are used to pierce skin and suck blood.

Thorax – the middle part of an insect's body where the legs are attached.

Typhus – a killer disease that can be passed on to humans by flea bites.

Vibration – a quivering motion.

index

A

abdomen 6–7, 10, 30
acceleration 17, 30
adults 5, 19, 21, 28
antennae 6, 30
arachnids 26–27, 30
arthropods 5, 30

B

barbs 11, 30
bats 4–5, 14–15
bees 26
beetles 7
birds 5, 8–9, 25
bites 11, 23
Black Death 23, 30
blood
    diseases 12–13
    food 4, 10–11
    larvae 18
bloodsucking insects
    10–11, 24–27
bristles 7, 9, 21
bubonic plague 23, 30

C

cat fleas 5–9, 29
    cocoons 20–21
    head 10–11
    larvae 18–19
    mouthparts 11
    hosts 14–15
chiggers 25
chigoe fleas 24
cleanliness 29
cockroaches 19
cocoons 19–21, 28, 30
crab lice 25

D

digestive system 30

fleas 7
    tapeworms 9
diseases 12–13, 23, 27,
    30
dogs 5, 29
droppings 18–19

E

earthworms 27
ectoparasites 9, 30
eggs 18–19, 28, 29
endoparasites 9, 30
energy storage 17
exoskeleton 5, 29, 30
eyes 6

F

feet-bloodsuckers 24–25
female fleas 18, 24, 29
food 4, 10–11

G

grasshoppers 19

H

head 6–7, 10–11
headlice 23
hexapods 7
honeybees 26
horses 5
hosts 5, 8–9, 30
    blood 10–11
    detecting 20–21
    diseases 12–13
    humans 22–23
    larvae 18–19
    waiting period 14–15
humans 22–23
    bites 11, 23
    cat fleas 15
    cleanliness 29
    crab louse 25

jumping power 16–17

I

insects
    bloodsuckers 10–11,
    24–27
    development 19
    legs 7
    parasites 9
    understanding 5, 30

J

jiggers 24
jumping power 16–17,
    29

L

larvae 30
    chiggers 25
    fleas 18–19, 28
leeches 27
legs
    bristles 21
    insects 5, 7
    muscles 17
lice 23, 25, 30
lifecycle 28–29

M

mammals
    diseases 12–13, 23
    hosts 4–5, 8–9,
    14–15, 22–23, 30
    humans 11, 15–17,
    22–23, 25, 29
    see also cat fleas
mating 18
microbes 13, 23, 30
minibeasts
    parasites 9
    understanding 5, 31
    see also insects

mites 25, 26
mosquitoes 27
mouthparts 11
muscle power 17
myxomatosis 12–13, 31

N

nymphs 19, 31

P

parasites 4–5, 9, 24–27,
    30–31
pets see cat fleas; dogs
plague 13, 23, 30
predators 4
pupae 19–21, 28, 31
pupation 19–20, 21, 31

R

rabbit fleas 12–15
rat fleas 13, 23
rodents 5, 13, 23, 31
roosts 14–15, 31

S

senses 20–21
skeleton 5, 29, 31
spines 7, 9
springtails 7, 31
stick-tight fleas 11
storing energy 17
stylets 10–13, 31

T

tapeworms 9
temperature 21
thorax 6–7, 31
ticks 27
typhus 23, 31

V

varroa mite 26
vibrations 21, 31

W

wings 5

Contents

1 Manchester: Changing Fortunes............4

2 Past Times 6

3 Landscape and Climate.....................8

4 Natural Resources 12

5 The Changing Environment...............16

6 The Changing Population..................22

7 Changes at Home 26

8 Changes at Work 36

9 The Way Ahead 44

Glossary 46

Further Information 47

Index 48

1 Manchester: Changing Fortunes

Manchester is one of the UK's most popular cities, famous for Manchester United Football Club and music acts including Oasis and Simply Red. Its trendy shops and cafés bustle with life and its people represent all parts of UK society, from the ultra rich to the extremely poor. In 2002 Manchester was chosen to represent the UK by hosting the Commonwealth Games. This picture of Manchester in the twenty-first century is very different from the Manchester of the past.

During the Industrial Revolution (between 1750 and 1850) Manchester was at the centre of the textile industry for which the UK was world famous. In the 1760s the spinning of cotton was first mechanized, bringing great wealth to the city. By the early twentieth century, however, Manchester was losing its importance as countries developed their own industries using newer machinery and cheaper labour. Manchester's decline continued and after suffering heavy bombing during the Second World War (1939–1945) the city was slow to recover.

By the 1970s many traditional industries had closed and unemployment and poverty were major problems. Manchester set about redeveloping itself by improving transportation, renovating or replacing buildings, and establishing new industries to replace the old. Progress has been slow at times, but in the late 1990s Manchester emerged as an exciting new city ready to face life in the twenty-first century. The story of Manchester is by no means unique and is shared by many other parts of the UK as they adapt to changes at home and in the wider world.

▲ *The Manchester metro system has helped to revive the city centre by improving the transport network.*

▼ *Manchester City Hall and its council members are at the centre of efforts to reshape the city and its people for life in the 21st century.*

▲ *This map shows the main geographical features of the UK, as well as most of the places mentioned in this book.*

THE UNITED KINGDOM: KEY FACTS

Area: 244,820 sq km

Population: 58.8 million

Population density: 240 people per sq km

Capital: London (7.6 million)

Other main cities: Birmingham (2.3 million), Manchester (2.2 million), Edinburgh (0.45 million), Cardiff (0.3 million), Belfast (0.28 million)

Highest mountain: Ben Nevis (1,343 m)

Longest river: Severn (338 km)

Main languages: English, Welsh (about 26 per cent of the population of Wales), Scottish form of Gaelic (about 1.2 per cent in Scotland)

Major religions: Christian (72 per cent), Muslim (2.7 per cent), Hindu (1 per cent), Sikh (0.5 per cent), Jewish (0.5 per cent), no religion (15.5 per cent), other (7.8 per cent)

Currency: British pound (1 pound = 100 pence)

2

Past Times

The UK is made up of England, Scotland, Wales and Northern Ireland. Northern Ireland is separated from the other three countries (known collectively as Great Britain) by the Irish Sea. Although it is relatively small, the UK was once the world's greatest economic and military power. When at its strongest in the late nineteenth century, the British Empire controlled vast areas of the globe including Australia, Canada, India and Kenya. In the first half of the twentieth century however, the UK suffered major population and financial losses as a result of two World Wars and the Great Depression. By the end of the Second World War (1945), it could no longer afford to maintain and control its empire and most British colonies gradually gained their independence. After 1945 countries such as the USA, Japan and Germany emerged as stronger and wealthier economies than the UK.

Since 1945 the UK has rebuilt itself and restructured its economy. Heavy industries (steel) and manufacturing (textiles) have declined and been replaced by service industries such as banking, leisure and education.

▲ *A war memorial reminds passers-by of the many people who gave their lives during two World Wars in order to protect the UK.*

▼ *The Houses of Parliament in London have overseen many historic changes in the UK.*

The UK has also formed new political and economic partnerships with its neighbouring countries by joining the European Union (EU) in 1973. This means that many EU policies now have an influence on British life, but in other ways the UK remains largely independent. For example, it decided not to adopt the new European currency (the Euro) when it was introduced in 2002. In 1999 the UK began a process called devolution that gives Scotland, Wales and Northern Ireland greater powers to manage themselves. How devolution will affect the future of the UK remains unclear, but one thing is certain, it will lead to yet more change.

▲ *The new Welsh Assembly in Cardiff has more control of Welsh affairs following devolution in 1999.*

IN THEIR OWN WORDS

'My name is Kirsty Williams and I am an Assembly Member (AM) of the Welsh Assembly that came into power in 1999 as part of the devolution process. Devolution means I have greater powers to work for the people who voted for me here in Brecon and Radnorshire. It gives people in Wales greater control over the things that matter to them most. With my party, the Liberal Democrats, I have helped to provide funding for Welsh university students and improved local healthcare. I am also working with local businesses and farmers to help promote everything that Wales has to offer to the UK and the wider world.'

3

Landscape and Climate

The UK covers a total area of 244,820 sq km and is a little under half the size of France or slightly smaller than the US state of Oregon. Located in the Atlantic Ocean, Great Britain (the UK without Northern Ireland), is the world's eighth largest island. The most obvious physical feature of the UK is its jagged coastline which extends for a total distance of 12,429 km. Wherever you stand in the UK you are never more than 120 km from the coast.

▲ *Giant's Causeway in Northern Ireland is one of the most dramatic parts of the UK coastline. The unique hexagonal rock formations were formed by the sudden cooling of volcanic lava as it erupted through the sea bed.*

Highs and lows

The UK landscape is surprisingly varied, ranging from the heights of Ben Nevis (1,343 m) in the Grampian Mountains of Scotland to the lowland Fens of England which are at or below sea level in places. Scotland and Wales are the most mountainous parts of the UK, with a ridge of hills, the Pennines, also running down the centre of northern England. Many coastal areas are low-lying, especially in the east and south of England. These include the wetlands of the Somerset levels, that regularly flood during heavy rains.

◄ *The Somerset levels in the south-west of England are one of the lowest-lying places in the country.*

IN THEIR OWN WORDS

'I'm Ian Jenkins and I'm one of 4,500 volunteers working for the Royal National Lifeboat Institution (RNLI). The RNLI is a charity funded by donations from the public. We have 224 lifeboats around the UK's coastline and make around 6,300 rescues a year. Since the RNLI began in 1824 we have saved almost 136,000 lives. Because people have greater leisure time more people are using the United Kingdom's coastline for activities such as sailing or windsurfing. The coast is very beautiful, but it can be dangerous if people don't take care. In recent years almost half of our rescues have been to pleasure craft that are in trouble. I'd like the government to help fund the work the RNLI does in safeguarding the UK coastline.'

The rest of the UK is made up of gently rolling hills with isolated areas of high ground such as Dartmoor in the south-west of England or the Mourne Mountains in Northern Ireland. Northern Ireland is also home to the UK's largest lake, Lough Neagh, which covers an area of 396 sq km. Other major lakes include Windermere in the English Lake District and Loch Lomond in Scotland. Another of Scotland's lakes, Loch Ness, is famous for sightings of 'Nessie', a mythical monster!

▶ *These green and gently rolling hills of Devon are typical of much of the UK's landscape.*

UK rivers

Being a relatively small island, the UK's rivers are not very long. The Severn, its longest river, is just 338 km in length, beginning in Wales and entering the Atlantic Ocean near Bristol. Other major rivers include the Thames, which flows through Oxford and London, and the Trent and Mersey rivers, which drain rainfall from large areas of central England.

◄ *The Thames, here flowing through central London, has long been important for trade and industry in the UK. The new housing on the riverside is a huge change in the last few years.*

Mild and varied

The UK's climate varies greatly according to season and location, but on the whole can be described as mild with few extremes. Winds and rains most often come from the Atlantic Ocean and so the west is generally wetter than the east. Rainfall is also greater on higher ground. For example, the highlands of western Scotland and Wales receive over 2,000 mm of rain per year, compared to lowlands in the south and east of England with less than 700 mm. Temperatures are generally warmer in the south than the north, but the greatest variation is between the winter months (November – March) and the summer months (June – August). In January average daily temperatures range from –1°C in the Scottish highlands to 5-6°C on the south coast whilst in July the average daily temperatures rise to 10°C and 16°C respectively.

▼ *Wales, in the west of the UK, experiences more rain than the central and eastern parts of the UK.*

In recent years the UK has experienced several extreme climatic events. Long wet periods have caused flooding and dry periods have occurred which have led to water shortages. The UK has been getting warmer with 1999 and 2002 being two of the warmest years since records began in 1659. Some scientists believe this is due to global climate change caused by pollution warming the Earth's atmosphere.

▶ *These bathers at Lyme Regis on the south coast are quick to enjoy the sunshine when it arrives.*

IN THEIR OWN WORDS

'My name is Anneliese Woodham and after studying meteorology at university I work as a weather presenter for a local radio station. It is beautiful and sunny today, but it is very hard to predict the UK's weather. Even with all the latest satellite technology we have, we can only look about three days ahead with any certainty. Even then we can still get it wrong! The British people are very interested in the weather because it can change so quickly. Some of the latest concerns are about global warming and the effect that it might have on our weather. We can expect warmer temperatures, but unfortunately we are also likely to have more flooding.'

Natural Resources

Energy rich

The most important natural resources in the UK are its energy resources which generate around 10 per cent of the UK's income (Gross domestic Product - GDP). Coal was the energy behind the Industrial Revolution and until 1900 the UK was the world's largest producer of coal.

It was still third largest in 1970 (behind the USA and China), but coal production has been in decline ever since. In 2000 it produced only 35 million tonnes of coal, compared to 145 million tonnes in 1970. The rising costs of extracting coal, concern about the harmful environmental impacts, and competition from other energy sources are the main reasons for the decline in coal production.

Oil and gas were discovered in the UK under the North Sea during the 1960s and new supplies are still being found today. Gas has been particularly important in replacing coal as a fuel for generating electricity. Between 1990 and 1999 the amount of UK electricity generated using gas increased from 1 to 34 per cent. In contrast, the amount of electricity produced using coal fell from 65 to 33 per cent.

▶ *Gas flares from an oil platform in the North Sea – the North Sea is the UK's main source of fossil fuels today.*

Renewable resources

Coal, oil and gas are all fossil fuels that are non-renewable and cause harm to the environment by releasing pollutants when they are burned. Because of this, the UK is developing alternative energy sources based on renewable energy. Wind energy is especially significant as the UK is the windiest country in Europe with enough wind to supply twice the UK's current electricity demand. In early 2003, the UK had just over 1,000 wind turbines providing around 0.3 per cent of UK electricity.

▶ *Wind turbines provide one of the most promising sources of renewable energy for the UK's future energy needs.*

IN THEIR OWN WORDS

'I'm James Woodley and I work for a small company that advises on the use of wind turbines to produce electricity for the UK. It is my job to look for the best sites to locate wind farms. The best locations in the UK are around its coastlines or on high ground. This means Wales and Scotland are particularly well suited, but other parts of the UK also have great potential. The biggest problem we face is that people don't want giant wind turbines near their homes and so permission is often blocked by local residents. Despite this, the clean energy from wind turbines is very promising and the best thing is that after the installation costs, wind is free.'

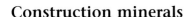

Construction minerals

Besides energy resources, the UK's other main commercial minerals are those used in the construction and building industries such as sand and gravel, limestone and gypsum. These are normally mined from the surface in quarries using heavy machinery. Smaller quarries are also found across the UK and provide stone for the local building industry. This means many parts of the UK have a distinctive appearance according to the locally available stone.

◄ *Small quarries such as this help to preserve traditional British skills such as stone masonary by providing them with a regular supply of material.*

▼ *The UK has a highly mechanised farming system, which means relatively few people are employed in agriculture.*

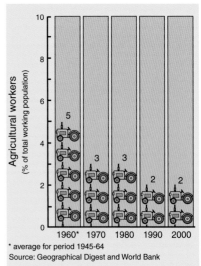

Of land and sea

The land and seas of the UK are its other main resource and support several of the country's most important industries including agriculture and tourism. Agriculture provides around 60 per cent of the UK's food needs even though it employs just 2 per cent of the country's labour force. UK agriculture is under pressure to change at the moment. Farmers are under pressure to adopt more environmentally friendly methods such as organic farming. Organic farming does not use artificial chemicals that can damage the environment and human health. Its popularity has grown rapidly with the number of organic farms increasing from just 1,000 in 1998, to 3,865 by early 2003. The fishing industry also faces problems. Many fish stocks have reached dangerously low levels because of over-fishing, which means the fish have not had a chance to breed and replace those that are caught.

The UK's land and coasts are also an important resource for attracting millions of tourists every year. Many of its most beautiful landscapes are today protected as national parks, such as Snowdonia in Wales and the Peak District in northern England. Several new national parks are being introduced from 2002 onwards, including the New Forest in southern England and Loch Lomond, the Trossachs and the Cairngorms in Scotland.

▲ *The South Downs on the south coast of England attract around 32 million visitors a year and will soon become a national park.*

IN THEIR OWN WORDS

'I'm Henry Kinge and I run a 4,000 acre farm in East Anglia. Farming is an ancient use of land in the UK, but is now experiencing some major changes. I used to run my farm like an industry, ripping out hedges and using machinery and chemicals to improve my harvest. Now I realize that we must manage the countryside for future generations and I am converting my farm to use organic methods. I am also replanting hedgerows to encourage wildlife back on to my land. Consumers want organic food because it helps to protect the environment, but they are not always happy to pay the higher prices. Overall though, organic farming has to be better for us all in the long run.'

5

The Changing Environment

Waste mountains

One of the biggest environmental challenges for the UK is how to deal with its growing waste problem. The main problems are dealing with the amount of waste that is generated and how to dispose of it. In 2001, UK households produced around 25 million tonnes of waste or about one tonne per household. The amount produced is increasing too, by about 3–4 per cent a year. Most household waste (around 78 per cent) is dumped in landfill sites and then buried. The problem is that it contains materials such as metals, glass and plastics that will take hundreds of years to break down and may also contain toxic substances that could pollute local soils and water supplies. Many UK landfill sites are almost full and new ones are becoming harder to find due to protests from people living close to planned sites. One option is to burn waste in incinerators and use the heat produced to generate electricity. But burning waste releases air pollutants, some of which have been linked to cancer in people.

▲ *Landfill sites may put waste out of sight, but they are not a solution to the UK waste problem.*

▶ *Most towns today have recycling facilities for items such as paper, glass and clothing.*

More recycling

The government aims to encourage households to recycle more of their waste. In 2001, just 12 per cent of household waste was recycled or composted. The government hopes to increase this to 45 per cent by 2015 by improving recycling facilities and educating people about the benefits of recycling. In Northern Ireland a 'Wake up to Waste' campaign was launched in February 2002. Using radio, television and a website to provide information to residents, recycling rates increased by up to 30 per cent in just a few months.

▲ *In some areas even garden waste is being recycled.*

IN THEIR OWN WORDS

'My name is Lin Li (right) and this is my friend Lu Zheng. We are originally from China, but are living in Brighton to complete our studies. One thing I have noticed since living here is the problem of waste and recycling. People seem to create a lot of waste with everything being wrapped or packaged. Why do supermarkets wrap up vegetables like cucumbers or peppers, it's just stupid! There are now recycling facilities in most places and where we live they also collect recycled waste from the kerbside. People should use these more and they should also buy goods and produce that use as little packaging as possible. This would help reduce the amount of waste created in the first place.'

Urban sprawl

The proportion of the UK population living in urban areas has increased slowly, rising from 84 per cent in 1950 to 90 per cent by 2001. However, the actual population of urban areas increased by around 9 million people over the same period – equivalent to the population of Sweden in 2002. As a result of this growth the UK's urban areas are rapidly sprawling (spreading) into their surrounding environments. In England, an average of 7,000 hectares of farmland, countryside and green space were converted to urban use every year between 1985 and 1998. This is almost the size of 9,600 international football pitches!

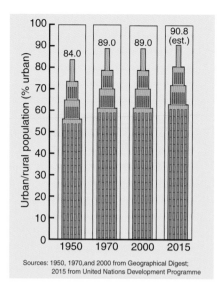

Sources: 1950, 1970, and 2000 from Geographical Digest; 2015 from United Nations Development Programme

▲ Most of the UK population lives in urban areas and the proportion living in rural areas is still declining slowly.

◄ In the Midlands, urban sprawl is becoming a problem.

In 2000, the UK government introduced regulations to encourage the building of homes within existing urban areas using 'brownfield sites' – land that has previously been built on. They also said that 30–50 houses should be built per hectare, an increase on the average of 25 houses per hectare being built in 1997–2001. Such measures are intended to better protect the countryside, reduce urban sprawl and regenerate urban centres.

▼ The Waterfront theatre in Belfast is built on the old dockside. Such projects make use of existing urban space and avoid sprawl.

Car culture

As urban areas have spread, people have switched from using public transport to using their own cars instead. This has resulted in traffic congestion and air pollution from motor vehicles. Cars, vans and taxis were used for around 85 per cent of all passenger journeys in 2001. The number of cars on the UK's roads has also increased dramatically, from almost 10 million in 1982 to 25.1 million in 2001. As urban centres grind to a halt because of traffic and congested roads, finding alternatives to the car is a key challenge.

▶ *Traffic congestion on the motorway network is one of the more visible environmental problems in the UK.*

IN THEIR OWN WORDS

'I'm Winston Major and I work for a metro system in the north of England. The metro has helped us to tackle the problem of growing traffic congestion by persuading people to leave their cars at home. There are still many people who refuse to use public transport though. They think of it as expensive or inconvenient because it does not run from outside of their door. We have to change this attitude in the UK and get people to use public transport more. Goods could also be transported better using the rail network instead of clogging the roads with lorries. The government should help to fund these changes as they do in Europe.'

Paying the price

Across many parts of the UK the environment has been paying the price for the successes enjoyed by the UK economy. Land has been built on, habitats such as forests and hedgerows have been removed, and rivers, lakes and the air have been polluted. UK wildlife has been some of the worst affected. Otters and salmon have vanished from many UK rivers where they once thrived.

▲ *More people are enjoying the UK's natural landscape, but this can cause problems such as erosion here in the Brecon Beacons National Park, Wales.*

Managing the environment

The government now realizes the amount of damage being caused and are introducing measures to manage the environment better. This has been helped by the fact that environments and wildlife are increasingly popular as major tourist attractions and so have widespread public support for their protection. The Peak District National Park in northern England is the second most visited park in the world (after Mount Fuji in Japan) with over 22 million day visits a year.

▶ *Many natural environments are protected thanks to their popularity for leisure activities such as this course for mountain bike races.*

IN THEIR OWN WORDS

'My name is Craig Earl and I'm a warden for the Forestry Commission in the UK. I trained in countryside management and spent some time working in national parks in Australia before returning to the UK. I think it is important to protect the UK's natural and man-made environments and to manage them for future generations. The forest here should be a place for everyone to enjoy. My job is to get people involved and to make them more aware. I help to organize events in the forest such as mountain biking or guided walks and we also encourage schools to visit us and learn about environmental management. It is important that future generations get involved at an early age.'

The UK is today focusing on policies that protect the environment for future generations whilst still promoting economic growth. This idea is known as sustainable development. In London, a system of congestion charging was introduced in 2003 where people are charged each day if they choose to drive into the centre of London. Congestion charging has proved successful so far and the number of cars entering the city centre has been reduced. If the scheme continues to be successful this will not only cut air pollution, but also help the city to run more efficiently by reducing the time wasted in traffic jams.

Other policies have included tighter controls on pollution in UK rivers. By 2001 otters were again seen in rivers in London, Birmingham, Glasgow and Newcastle, many for the first time since the 1970s.

▼ *A vehicle enters the congestion charging zone in London. Drivers must pay in advance and vehicles are monitored by traffic cameras.*

6 The Changing Population

Boom and stability

The UK population is today fairly stable at 58.8 million in 2001 and growing at just 0.28 per cent per year. In the 1950s and 1960s, however, the UK experienced a rapid rise in population that became known as the 'baby boom'. The baby boom was caused by improved economic and living conditions and the need to repopulate the UK following the deaths of so many people during the Second World War (1939–1945). In the 1950s and 1960s the UK population increased by almost 5 million, compared to just over 3 million between 1970 and 2001.

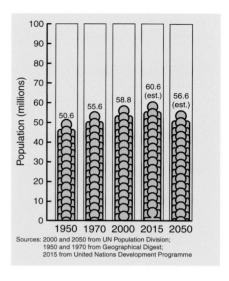

Sources: 2000 and 2050 from UN Population Division; 1950 and 1970 from Geographical Digest; 2015 from United Nations Development Programme

▲ *The UK population is expected to peak around 2015 and begin to decline by the middle of the century.*

Ageing

One of the most important changes in the UK population is its ageing. Life expectancy at birth increased dramatically in the last century from just 47 in 1901 to 78 in 2000. This means the number of elderly people (over the age of 65) in the UK is rising rapidly. In 2001 there were 9.4 million people over the age of 65, over 3 million more than

◄ *These elderly people enjoy a day out in Brighton. Older people make up an increasing proportion of the UK population.*

forty years earlier. As the baby boom generation grows older this number is expected to increase further still and reach almost 13 million by 2025. The elderly will also make up a bigger proportion of the population and by 2025 could make up 20.5 per cent of the population compared to 16 per cent in 2001. The ageing UK population is expected to cause serious social problems in the future, such as an increased demand for healthcare and a shortage of workers to support the ageing population.

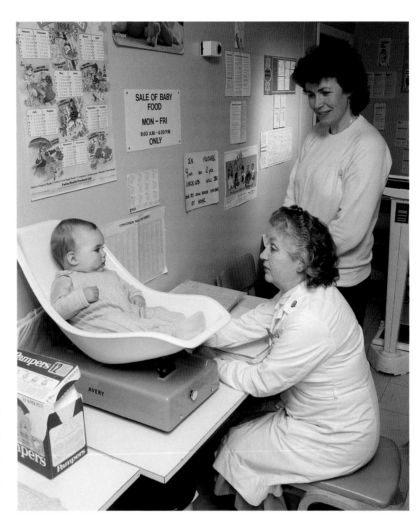

▶ *The National Health Service (NHS) provides free healthcare in the UK, but is under pressure from the changing demands of the population.*

IN THEIR OWN WORDS

'My name is Rogina Begum and I came to the UK from Bangladesh when I was just 9 years old. My parents had both died so I came to the UK with my uncle and his family. My uncle arranged my marriage to another immigrant from Bangladesh and we have one young son who is cared for by my uncle's family when I am working. Arranged marriages are not all bad as some people think. Anyway, I have a much wider choice as things are very different now. If my parents were still alive I don't think they would understand the way we live now. We have much more choice about when we have a family, how many children to have and whether we work or not.'

Ethnic diversity

The UK is today a multicultural society that is home to people from many different ethnic backgrounds. In total, people from ethnic groups other than white made up around 8 per cent of the UK population in 2001, or 4.6 million people. People of Asian origin make up half of the UK's ethnic minority population, with those of mixed ethnic origin or Black Caribbean and Black African origins being the other major groups. The distribution of ethnic minorities around the UK is extremely varied. The majority live in England and are centred around London (45 per cent) and the West Midlands (13 per cent). Scotland, Wales and Northern Ireland are home to the smallest ethnic minority populations, sharing less than 4 per cent of the UK total in 2001.

▲ *Stamford Hill in London, like many neighbourhoods, has an increasingly multicultural population.*

IN THEIR OWN WORDS

'I'm Ram Chanann and I'm a youth worker in Stirling, Scotland. Most of my work is with teenagers from poorer communities. They are often bored, with little to do and so we try to organize activities for them such as biking, canoeing or mountaineering. I came to the UK from Uganda and there are relatively few black people like me living in Scotland. On the whole I experience no problems being from an ethnic minority, but there are always some who make trouble. They do not seem happy to accept that the UK is now one of the most multicultural countries in the world. Thankfully people with such views are a minority themselves and so I am able to get on with my life contributing to my community like everyone else.'

Immigration and asylum

Many of the UK's ethnic minorities are descendants of people who were invited to migrate to the UK during the 1960s. They came mainly from former UK colonies such as India, Jamaica and Nigeria to take up jobs and help rebuild the UK economy. Today they have a major influence on many aspects of UK life such as food, music, clothing and religion. For example, curry, a dish originating from India, is today considered the UK's favourite food.

Today, the UK is faced with a growing number of uninvited or illegal immigrants. Many of them are seeking asylum and believe they have the right to stay in the UK because their lives are in danger in their country of origin. In 1996 there were around 30,000 asylum seekers, but by 2002 this had risen to over 110,000.

▼ *Many asylum seekers and illegal immigrants enter the UK hidden in lorries that use ports such as Dover on the south coast.*

▼ *Today, the UK is a multicultural society. This family are of West Indian origin.*

7

Changes at Home

Family structure

The once-typical UK family headed by two parents has undergone substantial changes during the late twentieth century. In particular there has been a rise in the number of single-person households, which increased from 18 to 29 per cent of all households between 1971 and 2002. This is explained by an increase in elderly people living alone and by more young people choosing to live alone and marry later in life. In England and Wales the average age at which people first marry increased by five years between 1961 and 2000 to just over 29.

More people are also choosing to live together (cohabit) without marrying. In 2000, around a quarter of unmarried people between the ages of 16 and 59 were cohabiting in Great Britain. Cohabiting couples are also starting families without first being married. Before 1960 this was very unusual, but in 2001 around 23 per cent of births in the UK were to cohabiting couples.

▲ Some couples decide to concentrate on their career before having a family.

◄ Many couples are enjoying a higher standard of living by choosing to have their families later in life.

IN THEIR OWN WORDS

'My name is Helen Hoff and I am a working mum with a young daughter, called Kaitlin, who is now three. When Kaitlin was born my partner and I were not married, but were cohabiting. When she was about one we decided to get married because we could then get more financial help from the government to help care for Kaitlin. Despite this, it is still very expensive to bring up a child today. Over half of my wage goes to pay for Kaitlin's childcare. I have friends who are single mums and struggle to get by. The government should do more to support young mums who want to work.'

Single parents

Another change in UK families has been the rise of single-parent families. This is largely due to more marriages ending in divorce, but some women are also choosing to have children as lone parents without being married. In 2001, single-parent families with dependent children (those under 16 or 16–18 and in full-time education) were fewest in England where they made up around 6.4 per cent of households and highest in Northern Ireland at 8.1 per cent of households.

▶ *Despite changing home lives in the UK, caring for children is still mainly done by women.*

Growth in housing

Because of changing family structures, the number of households increased by almost a third since 1971 to reach 25 million by 2001. More people are buying their own homes than in the past, too. In 2001 around 70 per cent of homes were owned with the remainder being rented properties.

◀ *This new housing development in Surrey in southern England will be unaffordable for many first-time buyers.*

One of the biggest problems in the UK is the growing cost of buying a home. In 1989 first-time buyers paid an average of around £40,000, but by 2001 this had more than doubled to £85,000. The cost of housing also varies dramatically around the UK from an average of £182,000 in London to £70,000 in the north-east of England. Housing in Scotland, Wales and Northern Ireland is on average around £37,000 cheaper than in England. The cost of housing in the UK has increased much faster than people's wages. The average annual wage in the UK in 2003 was around £20,000, whilst the average home was over £120,000.

▼ *Typical residential homes, such as these in Luton, can vary in price dramatically depending where they are in the UK.*

Religion

Christianity is the UK's main religion, followed by around 72 per cent of the population in 2001. Islam and Hinduism are followed by around 3 and 1 per cent of the population respectively. In 2001 about 15 per cent of the population had no religious beliefs. In Northern Ireland religious divides between Protestant Christians (who wish to remain part of the UK) and Catholic Christians (who wish to merge with the Republic of Ireland) have led to violent disputes since the 1960s. By the late 1990s the two sides were co-operating to share power in Northern Ireland, but in October 2002 co-operation collapsed, leaving an uncertain future.

▲ *This Hindu Swaminarayan temple in London was opened in 1996. It is said to be the largest in the western world.*

IN THEIR OWN WORDS

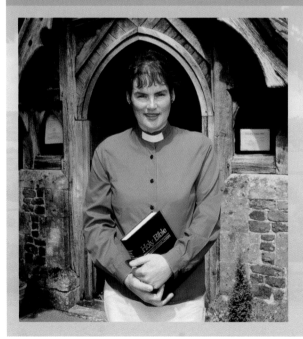

'I'm Sophie Jelly and I am a vicar. People think the church is less popular today, but I believe that people simply have more commitments than in the past. We are trying to make the church more approachable by working more closely with local communities. The church is also more friendly to young people than when I first started going to church. Some church groups even use pop-style music as part of their services. There are more women vicars and priests too. I think this encourages women to become more involved. The most important thing for the future is to make people feel welcome by the church. The church is much more than a building you go to on a Sunday.'

Health

As a nation the UK's health has improved dramatically over the last 100 years. People born in 2001 can expect to live 31 years longer than those born in 1901. The main health problems in the UK include heart disease, strokes, cancers and respiratory (breathing) diseases.

Lifestyle and diet

Many of the UK's health issues are related to lifestyle choices such as diet, cigarette and alcohol consumption, and exercise. Smoking was the cause of 120,000 deaths (20 per cent of all deaths) in 1995. Government campaigns warning of the dangers of smoking have helped to reduce the proportion of people regularly smoking in Great Britain from 46 per cent in 1974 to 27 per cent in 2000. Poor diets, such as those high in sugars and fats, are also related to many serious illnesses. In 2000 the UK government launched a campaign to improve people's diets by encouraging them to eat more fruit and vegetables. The aim is for people to eat five portions of fruit or vegetables a day.

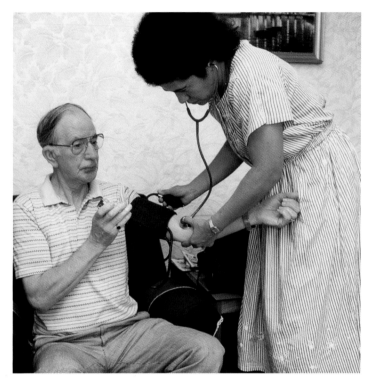

▼ *Better healthcare means British people are living longer and are healthier than at any time in the past.*

◀ *Young children are being encouraged to eat more fruit. From 2004 all children between the ages of 4 and 6 will be given a free piece of fruit, daily, by their school.*

IN THEIR OWN WORDS

'I'm Ivy Ford and I've been a school dinner lady for 23 years now. In that time I have seen many changes in children's diets. When I began working we used to make fresh food every day and serve proper meals. Today much of the food we serve arrives as frozen portions from an off-site kitchen. We simply heat them up and serve them. Pizza, pasta and sausage rolls are the favourites. We always offer at least two vegetables and salads and fruit too to try and encourage a more healthy and balanced diet. Many children now have a packed lunch instead but sometimes they are full of crisps and chocolates, which is not healthy for anyone!'

It is hoped that such measures will reduce problems such as obesity, which affects around 22 per cent of the UK population and has trebled since 1980. Despite government efforts, people are eating more processed foods and ready-made meals. Traditional meals such as fish and chips remain a UK favourite, but alternative fast foods such as burgers and pizzas are just as popular with today's young people.

▶ *Fish and chips remain a favourite meal for many British people.*

Improving education

Education is compulsory for all children in the UK between the ages of 5 and 16. At 16 students sit their General Certificate in Secondary Education (GCSE) examinations which provide them with the basic qualifications for their working life or further study. In 2001 around 75 per cent of people aged 16-18 chose to stay at school or college to take advanced-level examinations or vocational training courses that would prepare them for more specific jobs.

One of the biggest changes in education in recent years has been an increase in the number of students going to university. In 1994 around 271,000 students began a university course, but by 2001 this had increased by nearly a third to 358,000 students. In 2003 the government announced plans for further increases so that by 2010 half of all people aged 18-30 will enter higher education.

▲ *Home computers are becoming a new way for pupils to continue learning beyond the classroom.*

▼ *Belfast University has, like most others in the UK, seen its student numbers increase dramatically in recent years.*

IN THEIR OWN WORDS

'My name is Sam Enser and I'm just completing sixth form college where I am studying art, music, drama and music technology. Next year I'd like to study at a specialist art college, but because of the costs involved I will probably have to choose one that is close to home. That way I can stay living at home and save money on rent. My sister is just finishing her university degree. I don't think my parents could afford to fund us both in university at the same time. It will cost my parents and me at least £6,000 a year to go to university and like most students now, I will probably leave with large debts – it is a big worry for me.'

Education reform

The government is currently changing the UK education system to meet the future needs of the country. In schools new work-related subjects are to be introduced such as leisure and tourism, and information and communications technology. Existing subjects are also being adapted to cover important new issues such as sustainable development and citizenship. The government is also recruiting more teachers and allowing schools to specialize in areas such as technology or languages.

As new subjects have been introduced, however, the amount of sport in schools has declined. In primary schools the number of pupils doing two hours of sport a week in 1999 was down to 11–21 per cent, compared to 32–46 per cent in 1994. Sports authorities are concerned that the decline in sport could lead to higher levels of obesity in children.

▼ *Children have fewer opportunities to enjoy sports at school.*

Poverty and inequality

In 1999 the UK was ranked as the fifth richest country in the world. In the same year, however, 24 per cent of UK households were living in poverty. Although pockets of poverty exist across the UK it is possible to identify broad patterns of inequality. Southern and eastern areas of England are generally the wealthiest, whilst poverty is highest in northern England, Scotland, Wales and Northern Ireland. This has led many to talk about a north-south divide in the UK, but in reality patterns of poverty are more complicated than simply where people live. London, for example, has the UK's highest proportion of poor people, but also the second highest proportion of wealthy people, after Cheshire.

▲ *Leafy suburbs such as here in Winchester are typical of some of the wealthiest neighbourhoods in the UK.*

◄ *High-density flats such as these in South Wales are more frequently found in poorer parts of the UK.*

IN THEIR OWN WORDS

'I'm Rory McDowell and I'm 13. I live with my family in a high rise in Glasgow. My home is on the ninth floor, which is all right as long as the lift is working! It's not bad living here, although there are one or two gangs that cause problems from time to time. Most of them are involved in drugs, but I don't get involved – it's bad news. Instead I play football with my mates. I support Rangers. My dad used to work in shipbuilding, but it's all gone now and finding jobs is a real problem. My dad has no work and my mum works part-time in the chip shop. I'd like to train as a plasterer – there's better money in building.'

Social exclusion

A major concern in the UK is that poverty is excluding some people from the wider society. Ethnic minorities are particularly at risk from social exclusion. For example, they are more likely to suffer low incomes and difficulty in finding employment than the white community. In 2001, around two thirds of the Pakistani/Bangladeshi community were living in low-income households. People from Caribbean, African and Bangladeshi backgrounds find it twice as hard to get work as people of white origin.

In 1999 the government introduced several measures to reduce poverty and social exclusion, such as a national minimum wage and financial support for low-income families. By 2002 there were signs that poverty was falling, but there remained twice the number of people living on low incomes as in 1982.

▼ *People from ethnic minorities have been shown to suffer from greater social exclusion than others.*

8

Changes at Work

Industrial decline

Employment in the UK has seen major changes over the last 30 years or so as traditional industries such as manufacturing have closed or reduced in size. Employment in textile manufacturing fell from around 800,000 in the late 1970s to a little over 250,000 by 2001. The steel industry suffered an even bigger decline over the same period from around 150,000 to about 30,000. In fact the share of UK jobs in manufacturing fell by over half between 1978 and 2002 to 13.1 per cent.

Mining is another traditional industry that has undergone major changes. At the peak of UK coal mining in 1920 some 1.25 million miners were employed, but by 1950 this had fallen to around 700,000 as pits began to close. It was in the second half of the twentieth century that most closures happened, however, and by 1998 the UK had fewer than 9,000 coal miners.

▲ *Once at the heart of the Industrial Revolution, Ironbridge is today a popular tourist town with museums focusing on this important period in UK history.*

▼ *Many of the UK's coal mines have closed in recent decades. This derelict mine is in South Wales, an area badly affected by closures.*

IN THEIR OWN WORDS

'My name is George Millar, but my friends call me Geordie. I live here in Belfast and for 42 years I worked as a fitter for Harland and Wolfe, one of the biggest shipbuilding companies in the world. However, the shipbuilding industry declined and Harland and Wolfe closed, making workers like me redundant. The government should never have allowed the docks to close: we still have the skills in this country and could rebuild them. I am now a partner in a ship repair business. We maintain and repair the engines on cross-channel ferries and other ships. It pays well, but is not the same as the shipbuilding days. It's not right to just throw away an industry like that.'

Wider impact

With such enormous job losses, it is not just individual workers and their families that are affected. Whole communities have suffered following the closure of mines, factories or shipyards. This is because the lack of employment leads to a loss of income and a fall in demand for local services from shops to hairdressers. This is known as a knock-on effect. The impact is especially severe when closures take place suddenly and involve large numbers of workers. In 2001 the Llanwern steel works closed in Wales with the loss of around 3,000 jobs. A further 10,000 jobs in the surrounding area were said to be threatened by the closure.

▼ *Many of the cars bought in the UK today are manufactured overseas instead of in the UK.*

Services expand

The decline in employment in traditional industries has been more than matched by an increase in employment in the service sector. The service sector includes jobs such as those in banking, insurance, retail, restaurants, leisure, travel and tourism. Between 1978 and 2002, employment in the UK service sector increased by nearly 7 million jobs to make up 78.4 per cent of the workforce.

Jobs related to tourism and leisure have grown particularly fast in recent years as people have more disposable income (income after they have paid housing and other essential costs) to spend on enjoying themselves. Employment in restaurants increased by almost a quarter of a million people between 1992 and 2002 as people ate out more frequently. Other services benefited from an increase in the number of tourists visiting the UK which grew from 12.4 million in 1980 to 25.2 million by 2000 and is expected to increase further in the coming years.

▲ *The 'London Eye', a giant Ferris wheel alongside the Thames, is one of the country's top new tourist attractions.*

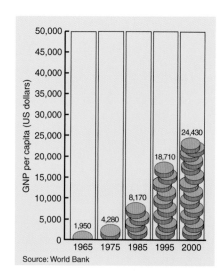

Source: World Bank

▶ *Average incomes in the UK have increased sharply since the 1990s. The UK is today one of the wealthiest countries in the world.*

IN THEIR OWN WORDS

'My name is Pat Hesketh and I'm a librarian in Belfast. In recent years we have been busy computerizing the library system. This means people can borrow books from anywhere in the region and don't have to travel to each individual library. We are also busy helping people to use the Internet, which is free to all library users. It is good for the library, because many people end up borrowing a book. Children are especially keen to use the Internet service. Many use it for their homework assignments. The information services that libraries now provide are an important public service and I'm proud to work for them.'

Retail boom

The retail sector in the UK has also grown rapidly with British people shopping more than ever before. Between 1986 and 2002 the volume of retail sales (not including food) increased by around 68 per cent, whilst their value increased by nearly 79 per cent. Sales of electrical and hi-tech items such as computers, game consoles and mobile phones have grown particularly fast. In 1986 just 4.8 per cent of people had a personal computer compared to 37 per cent in 2001. Ownership of mobile phones grew even faster from 0.2 per cent of the population in 1986 to almost 77 per cent in 2001.

▼ *Shopping centres such as this one in Kent provide thousands of jobs for local people.*

Technology at work

Technology such as the home computer, mobile phone and the Internet have introduced new methods of working in recent years. For example, many more people are now choosing to work from home and stay in touch with their office or colleagues and clients by telephone, e-mail, video-conferencing and the Internet. In 1981 there were just under 346,000 people who worked mainly from home, but by 1998 this had almost doubled to 681,000 or 2.5 per cent of the UK workforce.

▶ *New advances in technology make it possible for people to work from home.*

IN THEIR OWN WORDS

'I'm Ronnie Hutchinson and I'm a self-employed hairdresser. I used to work at a salon in London, but childcare was too expensive. Working from home allows me to manage my work and family life together. The government has made it reasonably easy to be self-employed as long as you keep good records for the tax office. Working from home causes a few problems though. For example I often work in the evenings after collecting my daughters from school, but this means I can't spend as much time with them. Some customers don't like to come to my home in the evening and so finding suitable times can be difficult. On the whole, though, working from home has given me much more freedom.'

◀ *Increasing numbers of nursery school places have helped many parents, especially women, return to work after starting their family.*

Employment changes

Most people who work full-time from home are also self-employed. Across the UK an estimated 3.1 million people were self-employed in 2002, or around 11 per cent of the working population. Though this has changed little since the mid-1980s, self-employment is expected to be one of the UK's fastest growing forms of employment in future years.

One of the most noticeable trends in employment in the UK has been an increase in the number of part-time jobs, especially in the retail industry. By 2002, 22.3 per cent of all those in employment were working part-time. Part-time jobs reflect changes in society as more people are mixing work with study or with caring for their families. Many part-time workers are women who have returned to work after having their families. In 2002, for instance, around 82 per cent of part-time workers were women.

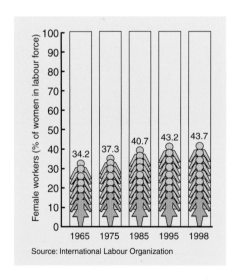

Source: International Labour Organization

▲ *The proportion of women in the UK labour force has increased by around ten per cent from 1965 to 1998 and continues to grow.*

The future of farming

In 1951 there were around 918,000 agricultural workers but this had more than halved to 422,000 by 2002 as machinery replaced workers and competition from abroad forced many farms to close. One of the biggest setbacks in recent years was an outbreak of foot and mouth disease in 2001, the first since 1967. Foot and mouth was started in 2001 by infected animal feed and spread quickly among livestock as they were moved between markets around the country. In order to control the spread of the disease the government ordered the slaughter of 4.2 million animals. The outbreak forced farmers and the government to question what the future of British farming would be. It is not yet clear what will happen as a result, but it is likely that organic farming will expand and that farmers will become involved in other activities such as using their land for leisure or tourist activities.

▲ *Dairy farming is coming under increasing pressure to become organic.*

◄ *Some farmers have taken to selling their produce directly to customers in regional farmers' markets.*

Twenty-first-century employment

At the start of the twenty-first century the employment situation in the UK was better than at any time since the early 1980s. Just 5.1 per cent of the workforce were unemployed in early 2003 – the lowest level for 25 years. As the job market continues to change, however, people will have to continue developing new skills and retraining if unemployment is to stay low. In particular there is a shift in demand from manufacturing skills towards skills based on information technology (IT) such as computers and the Internet. In 1992 around a quarter of people used IT in their jobs, but by 2000 this had risen to over 60 per cent and the need for IT skills is set to increase further in the coming years.

▼ *New offices provide space for the expected increase in UK service jobs in the future.*

IN THEIR OWN WORDS

'I'm Sam Bower and I'm a student, retraining in design technology. I didn't do very well in school and failed many of my exams. I then travelled in Europe for a little while because I was unsure what I wanted to do. I have always liked art and so decided to go into the design industry. Today, technology plays a major role in the design industry and much of the work is done using computers. I really enjoy what I'm doing and when I'm finished I would like to use my skills to work for an organization such as Oxfam. I'm proof that it is never too late to retrain for something you really want to do.'

9

The Way Ahead

Looking forwards

At the start of the twenty-first century the UK is at a crossroads in its history and development. It is leaving behind the traditional industries of the past and creating a new economy built around information technology and conducting business worldwide. It is also starting a new period in its political organization with Scotland, Wales and Northern Ireland being given increasing powers to manage themselves. The people of the UK are retraining and learning new skills to help the UK maintain its position as one of the world's most important economies.

▲ *Retail will continue to play a major role in the future of the UK economy.*

The UK still faces many problems, however. For example, its healthcare system is in need of major reform to meet the needs of its ageing population, and education must adapt to teach skills needed for success in the twenty-first century. The UK environment is also in need of greater care, and problems such as waste and transport are in need of urgent attention.

▶ *In the 1980s parts of east London were developed to provide modern facilities for new businesses.*

IN THEIR OWN WORDS

'My name is Daryl McMaster and I run an import business. I bring goods into the UK, mainly from China and India, and then export them again to our European neighbours. One of the biggest problems facing my business is the question of whether or not to join the euro. Because of changes in the value of the euro we can lose large sums of money on some of our business deals. The government must decide whether or not to join the euro currency soon. The uncertainty is very bad for small businesses like mine.'

The UK and Europe

One of the biggest questions for the future of the UK is how far it co-operates with its neighbours in Europe. In particular the UK must decide whether or not it wants the new European currency, the euro, that was adopted by 12 of the 15 countries in the European Union in January 2002. Many British people wish to keep the British pound and not become too involved with Europe. Others fear that the UK may get left behind. Whatever happens, the decision is sure to mark another stage in the continually changing face of the UK.

▼ *For these children growing-up in the twenty-first century will be an exciting and changing time.*

Glossary

Baby boom A period in UK history characterized by a high number of births and so a rapid growth in the population. Generally thought of as 1946–1964.

British Empire Countries and/or territories of the world that were once under the control of the UK.

Brownfield sites Land, normally within or surrounding urban areas, that has been previously built upon or used for a purpose other than farming.

Cohabit To share accommodation with another person. Normally used to describe adults who live together without first being married.

Colonies Countries that are occupied and politically controlled by other countries. The UK colonized many countries around the world up until the mid 1900s, such as Nigeria, Kenya and India.

Dependent children Those children who are dependent on their parents or carers to provide for them. In the UK considered to be children under 16 or under 18 if in full-time education.

Devolution A process in which part of a country is given greater control of its own affairs and the central government becomes less involved.

Ethnic Of or descending from a specific cultural group such as Asian or Caribbean. Often used to describe patterns of society.

European Union (EU) A political and economic union of 15 European countries. The UK joined the EU in 1973. From 2004 the EU will expand to include 13 other European nations.

Fossil fuels Fuels from the fossilized remains of plants and animals formed over millions of years. They include coal, oil and natural gas. Once used they are gone – they are non-renewable.

Great Depression A worldwide economic crisis that began in 1929 in the USA and lasted until 1933. Industries closed and millions of people lost their jobs. In the UK unemployment reached 3 million.

Habitat The place in which an animal or plant lives. For example, a squirrel lives in a woodland habitat.

Incinerator A furnace where waste is disposed of by burning it at high temperatures.

Independence When a country becomes free to form its own government and make its own decisions, independent of any other country that may have previously ruled over it.

Industrial Revolution The period in the late eighteenth century and early nineteenth century when new machinery and the use of fossil fuels to generate energy led to the start of modern industry and dramatic changes in the way people lived.

Knock-on effect When one event causes others to occur as a result. For example the closure of a factory and the loss of jobs could cause local shops to go out of business as people have less money to spend.

Landfill sites Holes or hollows in the ground used for burying waste from human activities.

Mechanized Using a machine to carry out tasks that would previously have been done by hand.

Non-renewable Resources that once used are gone and cannot be replaced except over millions of years. These include coal, oil and natural gas.

Organic farming Farming crops or raising livestock without using artificial chemicals. Yields are often lower, but organic produce is said to be safer for human consumption and less damaging to the environment.

Pollutants Any substance that pollutes another, for example, chemicals and waste products that contaminate the air, soil and water.

Recycle To collect and process used materials (e.g. glass, paper, cardboard and aluminium) so that they can be used again instead of being disposed of.

Renewable resources Resources that are easily replaced or replace themselves to be used again. The sun is a renewable energy resource because it can be reused every day, but coal or oil that takes millions of years to replace itself, is not.

Respiratory diseases Diseases that are associated with people's ability to breathe.

Social Exclusion Where circumstances prevent groups of people or individuals from joining in with the normal activities of the society in which they live.

Sustainable development Development that meets the needs of today without compromising the ability of future generations to meet their needs.

Toxic A poisonous substance which causes harm to human health and/or the environment.

Unemployment benefit A payment made by the government to people who are unable to find work.

Wetland An area of land dominated by water. It supports aquatic plants and animals.

Further Information

Books to read

United Kingdom by Rob Bowden (Evans Brothers, 2002)

Citizen's Guide To: the UK Economy by Sean Connolly (Heinemann Library, 2002)

Citizen's Guide To: Governing the UK by Ivan Minnis (Heinemann Library, 2002)

Useful addresses

Britain and London Visitor Centre
1 Regent Street
London
SW1Y 4XT

National Trust
UK Central Office
36 Queen Anne's Gate
London
SW1H 9AS

Association of National Park Authorities
126 Bute Street
Cardiff
CF10 5LE

Index

Page numbers in **bold** refer to photographs, maps or statistics panels.

agriculture *see farming*

Belfast **18**, **32**, 37, 39

childcare 23, 27, 40, 41, **41**
climate 10–11
coal mining 12, 36, **36**
coasts 8, 9, **11**, 15
communications 33, 39, 40
computers **32**, 39, 43
congestion charging 21, **21**
currency 5, 7, 45

devolution 7, 44

economy 6, 20, 22, 25, **38**, 44
education 32–3, **32–3**, 44
elderly people 22–3, 26
empire 6
energy 12–13
England **5**, 6, 8, 9, 10, 15, 18, 24, 26, 27, 28
environmental
    problems 12, 13, 16–21, 44
    protection 15, 20–21
ethnic minorities 24–5, 35
euro 7, 45
European Union (EU) 7, 45

family life 23, 26–7, 35, 40, 41
farming **14**, 14–15, 42, **42**
fishing 14
food and drink 30–31, **30–31**

gas 12, **12**
global warming 11

health 30–31, 33
healthcare 23, **23**, 30, **30**, 44
housing 18, **18**, 28, **28**, **34**, 35

immigration 23, 25
Industrial Revolution 4, 12, 36
industry 4, 6, 14, 36–7
information technology (IT) 3, 39, 40, 43

lakes 9
languages 5
lifeboats 9
life expectancy 22
London **5**, 6, 10, **10**, 21, **21**, 24, **24**, 28, **29**, **38**, **44**

Manchester 4, **4**, 5, **5**
manufacturing 6, 36, 37, 43
marriage 23, 26, 27
minerals 12, 14
mountains 5, **5**, 8, 9

national parks 15, **15**, 20, **20**, 21
Northern Ireland **5**, 6, 7, **8**, 9, 17, **18**, 24, 27, 28, 29, **32**, 34, 37, 39, 44

pollution 13, 16, 19, 20, 21
population 5, 22–5
    density 5
    growth 18, **18**, 22, **22**
poverty 4, 34–5

quarrying 14, **14**

recycling **16**, 17, **17**
religion 5, 29, **29**
renewable energy 13
rivers 5, **5**, 10, **10**, 21

Scotland **5**, 6, 7, 8, 9, 10, 15, 24, 28, 34, 44
self-employment 40, 41
service industries 6, 38–9
shipbuilding 35, 37
shopping 39, **44**
sport and leisure 4, 9, **20**, 33, **33**, 35, 38, 42
steel making 6, 36, 37

textiles 4, 6, 36
tourism 15, 20, **36**, 38, **38**, 42
transport 4, **4**, 19, **19**, 21, **21**, 44

unemployment 4, 35, 36–7, 43
urban growth 18, **18**

wages 28, 35
Wales **5**, 6, 7, 8, 10, **10**, 15, 24, 26, 28, **34**, 34, **36**, 37, 44
    Welsh Assembly 7, **7**
waste 16–17, 44
wind power 13, **13**
women in workforce 7, 11, 23, 27, 29, 31, 39, 40, 41, **41**
work
    from home 40, **40**
    part-time 41
World Wars 4, 6, **6**, 22

THE NUTCRACKER

Illustrated by Valeria Docampo

Based on the New York City Ballet production of *George Balanchine's The Nutcracker*®

SIMON AND SCHUSTER

London   New York   Sydney   Toronto   New Delhi

THE NUTCRACKER

SIMON AND SCHUSTER
First published in the USA in 2016 by Little Simon, an imprint of Simon and Schuster Children's Publishing Division, New York
This edition first published in Great Britain in 2016 by Simon and Schuster UK Ltd, 1st Floor, 222 Gray's Inn Road, London, WC1X 8HB
A CBS company
Copyright © 2016 by New York City Ballet Incorporated
All rights reserved, including the right of reproduction in whole or in part in any form
A CIP catalogue record for this book is available from the British Library
Printed in China
ISBN: 978-1-4711-6116-2 (HB)
ISBN: 978-1-4711-8711-7 (PB)
ISBN: 978-1-4711-6118-6 (eBook)
1 3 5 7 9 10 8 6 4 2

It was Christmas Eve at the Stahlbaums' house, and like children everywhere, Marie and Fritz were so excited that they could feel their toes tingle. Their parents were decorating the Christmas tree before the big holiday party, and Marie and Fritz were not allowed into the great room until it was done. They jostled each other to sneak a peek at the glittering tree through the keyhole.

At last the guests arrived, and the doors were thrown open. "Let the party begin!" everyone cried as they joyfully filled the festive room.

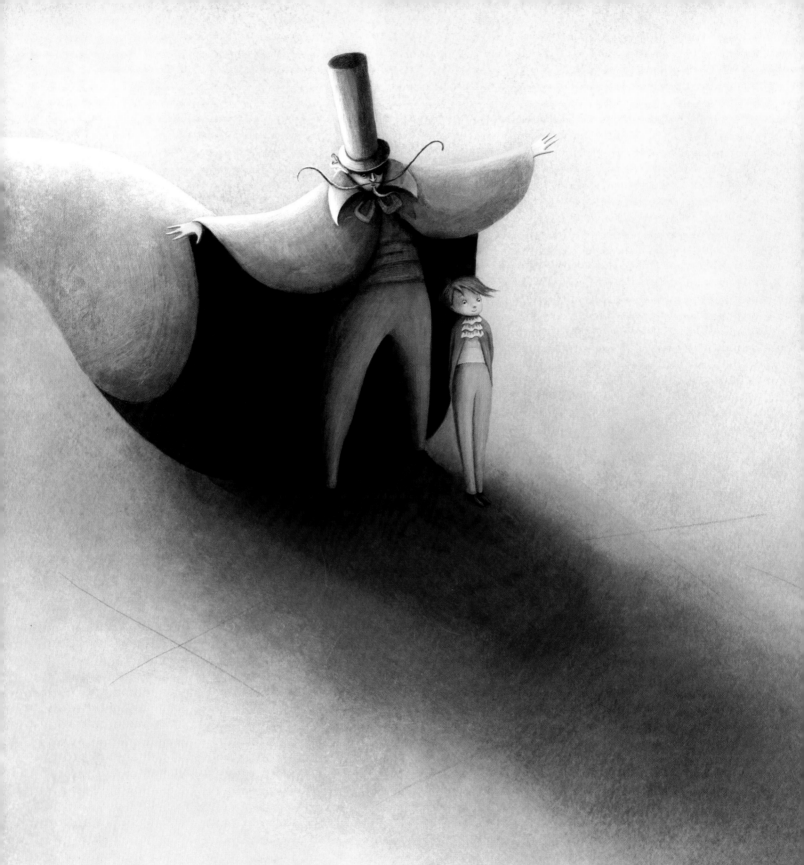

The children danced and played, and everyone was merry until . . .
the lights flickered and the room grew dark. A mysterious man with a
young boy entered from the shadows. The man was dressed all in black,
with a huge fluttering cape. The children scurried to hide behind their
parents just as he paused and flung back his cape over his shoulder.

Ah, there was nothing to fear. It was just Herr Drosselmeier, Marie's beloved godfather! Marie flew into his arms for a hug and shyly met his young nephew.

Herr Drosselmeier was a toy inventor, and a visit from him was always full of surprises. The curious children, their eyes full of wonder, gathered around three huge boxes he had brought with him. Suddenly the boxes sprang open, and out leaped one life-size doll, then another, and then another. The dolls danced for the delighted crowd.

As the celebration continued, Herr Drosselmeier beckoned to Marie. He had a special gift for her: a nutcracker! The Nutcracker was dressed as a handsome soldier with a white beard. Herr Drosselmeier showed Marie how the Nutcracker could open and snap his mouth to crack nuts for everyone. *Crack, crack!*

Marie was enjoying cracking nuts and passing them out to the children when suddenly jealous Fritz swooped in and snatched the Nutcracker from her. He swung it around the room and smashed it down onto the floor with a loud *bang*. Marie burst into tears. Her beloved Nutcracker was broken!

But Herr Drosselmeier knew just how to fix the Nutcracker. He tied a scarf around the Nutcracker's head like a bandage and handed him back to Marie, who cradled him in her arms. Then Herr Drosselmeier's nephew gave Marie a tiny bed that was the perfect size for a nutcracker, and Marie nestled him in it to rest.

The party was coming to a close, and everyone joined in for one last grand dance. When the music ended, the guests bundled up and made their way out into the frosty night air.

Marie waved goodbye to her dear godfather and his handsome nephew. It had been a long evening, and it was time for bed.

uring the night, Marie awoke, remembering that the Nutcracker was alone downstairs in his bed. She ran down to scoop him up. With the Nutcracker safely in her arms, she curled up on the sofa and drifted back to sleep in the soft glow of the Christmas tree.

She hadn't been asleep for long when Herr Drosselmeier slipped back into the house to properly mend the Nutcracker. He gently slid him out of Marie's arms, repaired him under the light of the moon, and disappeared into the darkness.

But then strange things began to happen. At the stroke of midnight, Marie was pulled from her sleep by the clock chimes. She rubbed her eyes in surprise. Great big mice appeared from the shadows and began to scurry across the room.

The lights were flashing brightly as it rose higher and higher.

With a rumble and a shake, the tree began to grow before her eyes.

Marie had never seen anything so big.

Then Fritz's toy soldiers sprang to life. They marched in to battle the mice. The mice were led by the fierce and terrible Mouse King, who wore a shiny crown on his head. Then the Nutcracker himself came to life, growing until he was the size of Marie. His bed, now huge, spun around and around.

The Nutcracker leaped out of the bed to lead the battle against the mice. The Mouse King towered over the Nutcracker, taunting him, when a quick-thinking Marie threw her slipper and it landed on the king's head. He turned to look away, and the Nutcracker toppled him over. The Nutcracker triumphantly claimed the Mouse King's crown in victory.

In that very moment, the ancient spell that had been cast on the Nutcracker was broken. He transformed into a handsome prince who looked very much like Herr Drosselmeier's nephew.

The Prince gallantly placed the crown on top of Marie's head and led her by the hand into the starry night, beyond her house and deep into the forest toward the Christmas Star. Snow began to fall, and the glistening flakes began to dance.

The Prince took Marie on a fantastic journey. They boarded a cosy walnut boat and sailed into the night, soon landing in an enchanted kingdom called the Land of Sweets. The Land of Sweets was a magical place filled with candy dripping in icing and magnificent, delicious colours as far as the eye could see.

News of their arrival travelled fast, and Marie and the Prince were greeted by the Sugarplum Fairy, who reigned over the land. She welcomed them with a curtsy, and with a wave of her sparkly wand, a host of delights from her kingdom appeared before them.

The Prince told the story of their great battle with the Mouse King.

"Oh, you are both very brave," the Sugarplum Fairy said. Then she invited them to celebrate by settling in two magnificent candy thrones, with big bowls of chocolate, cake, and ice cream set before them.

The Sugarplum Fairy summoned everyone in the Land of Sweets to dance for the Prince and Marie in honour of their victory.

First there was a delightful dance of spicy Spanish hot chocolate, heralded by the call of trumpets and snapping fingers.

Next came the mysterious Arabian coffee dance that ended with the tinkling of tiny cymbals, giving way to the explosive leaps and turns of Chinese tea.

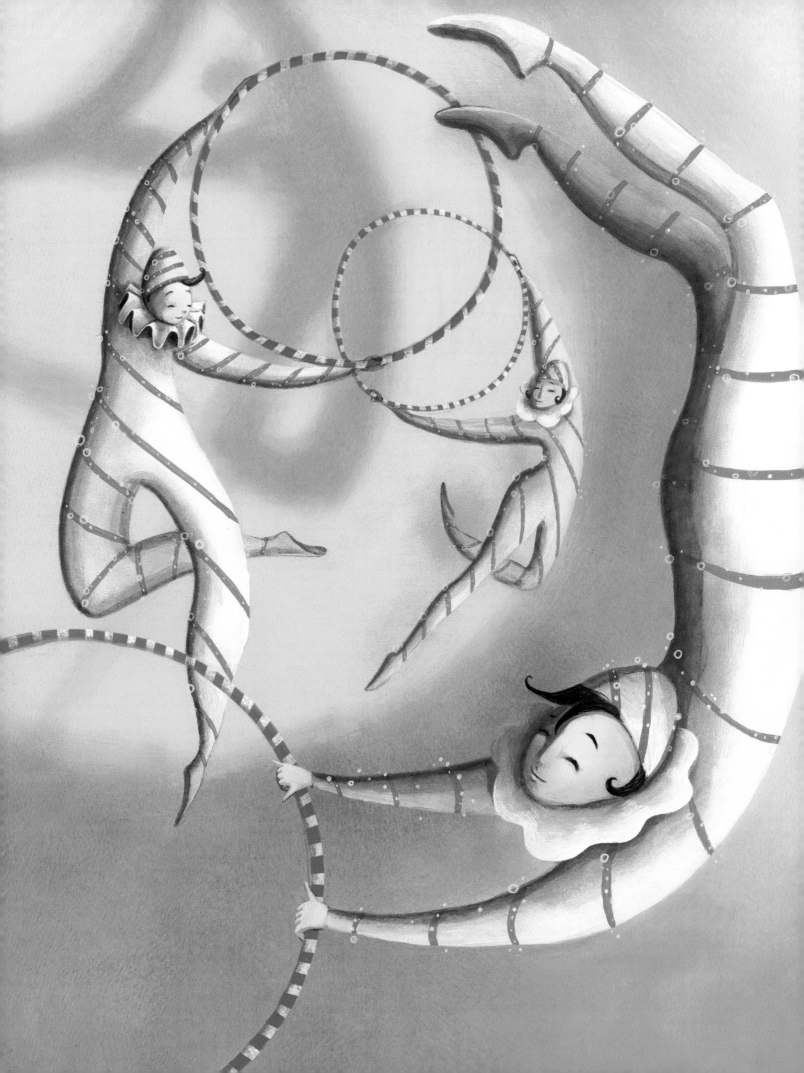

The jumping candy canes emerged next, leaping high into the air and dancing through hoops.

What could come after candy canes? Marzipan shepherdesses stepped out, tiptoeing delicately while playing their flutes.

The biggest surprise of all was the gigantic Mother Ginger, who swaggered before them. All of a sudden eight tiny clowns, called polichinelles, sprang from beneath her skirt and danced to the rhythm of her tambourine.

As Mother Ginger scooted her children off, a garden of flowers appeared. Amid the blooms was the shimmering Dewdrop Fairy, and with each step she brought every single petal to life in blossoming swirls of pink.

Finally, the regal Sugarplum Fairy returned with her noble cavalier.
They floated gracefully about, and then she spun faster and faster before
leaping into his arms. It was all so deliciously marvellous.

With another wave of her wand, the Sugarplum Fairy summoned her whole kingdom for a joyous farewell celebration.

As much as they wanted to stay, it was time for Marie and the Prince to leave the Land of Sweets and return to their families. As the lovely soft snow continued to fall, they climbed into a beautiful sleigh pulled by magical reindeer. Marie and the Prince turned to wave goodbye to their new friends as they rose higher and higher into the sky, away from their sweet celebration and into the starry night.

George Balanchine's THE NUTCRACKER® Fun Facts

- The Christmas tree grows to a full height of 41 feet and weighs 1 ton.

- 50 pounds of paper snow is used to create the snowstorm that ends the first act of the ballet.

- There are 144 jingle bells on each of the candy cane costumes.

- Mother Ginger's skirt weighs 85 pounds and is 9 feet wide.

- There are nearly 1 million watts of lighting used in the ballet's grand finale.

- Each performance features more than 50 dancers and more than 60 children from the School of American Ballet, the official school of NYCB.

- More than 150 costumes are worn by the cast.

- 62 musicians play in the orchestra.

The Nutcracker was created by composer Peter Ilyich Tchaikovsky and choreographers Marius Petipa and Lev Ivanov, and it was first performed at the Mariinsky Theatre in St. Petersburg, Russia, on 18 December 1892. The ballet was not initially considered a success.

George Balanchine, who was born in St. Petersburg in 1904 and performed in the *The Nutcracker* as a student at the Mariinsky Theatre, decided to choreograph his own version of the ballet as his first full-length work for New York City Ballet, which he had cofounded in 1948.

Premiering on 2 February 1954, Balanchine's production of *The Nutcracker* was an extraordinary success, and it helped to establish both the ballet and its score as perennial favourites around the world.

George Balanchine's The Nutcracker®
BALLET IN TWO ACTS, FOUR SCENES, AND PROLOGUE
Based on E. T. A. Hoffmann's tale *Nutcracker and the Mouse King* (1816)

Music by **Peter Ilyich Tchaikovsky**
Choreography by **George Balanchine***
Scenery by **Rouben Ter-Arutunian**
Costumes by **Karinska**
Original lighting by **Ronald Bates**
Lighting by **Mark Stanley**

*© The George Balanchine Trust

Premiere: 2 February 1954, New York City Ballet,
City Center of Music and Drama, New York

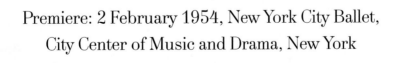

Learn more at **nycballet.com**.